Arno Clemens Gaebelein

The Seven Parables, Matthew XIII.

An exposition

Arno Clemens Gaebelein

The Seven Parables, Matthew XIII.
An exposition

ISBN/EAN: 9783744795524

Printed in Europe, USA, Canada, Australia, Japan

Cover: Foto ©Lupo / pixelio.de

More available books at **www.hansebooks.com**

The Seven Parables

MATTHEW XIII.

AN EXPOSITION

BY

A. C. GAEBELEIN

Editor of "Our Hope"

With the Compliments of

THE BIBLE HOUSE OF LOS ANGELES

505 MASON BUILDING

LOS ANGELES . . . . . CALIFORNIA

GREETINGS

THE BIBLE HOUSE OF LOS ANGELES sends greetings to their fellow labourers in the Gospel, and have much pleasure in presenting this booklet, which is commended to your prayerful reading.

ADVISORY COUNCIL

OF

THE BIBLE HOUSE OF LOS ANGELES

(Formerly The Los Angeles Bible Institute)

REV. F. W. FLINT	*Christian Alliance*
MR. LYMAN STEWART	*Presbyterian*
REV. W. W. LOGAN	*United Presbyterian*
PROF. MELVILLE DOZIER	*Baptist*
MR. S. I. MERRILL	*Baptist*
REV. E. J. INWOOD	*Methodist Episcopal*
REV. W. P. HARDY	*Congregational*

OFFICERS

A. B. PRICHARD	*President*
MELVILLE DOZIER	*Vice-President*
R. D. SMITH	*Secretary-Treasurer*

Office: 505 Mason Building, Los Angeles, Cal.

Correspondence should be addressed to the Secretary.

THE SEVEN PARABLES.

I.

The thirteenth chapter in the Gospel of Matthew contains seven parables, which the Lord Jesus Christ uttered, after His people had rejected the message of the kingdom. This chapter is one of the greatest importance. It demands, therefore, our closest attention, and this more so because the revelation which our Lord gives here, the unfolding of the mysteries of the kingdom of the heavens, has been and still is grossly misunderstood and falsely interpreted. Precisely that which our Lord did not mean has been read into this chapter. The whole chapter has been, so to speak, turned upside down by most of the learned commentators of Christendom. For any believer to turn to these for light and instruction will only result in getting thoroughly confused. It may be said if this chapter would be rightly understood by the professing church, the consequences would certainly be the most far-reaching. But one almost despairs of seeing the true meaning of the mystery of the kingdom in Matthew xiii believed in Christendom. The professing church continues, and will continue, to build upon the misinterpretation of our Lord's parables the optimistic dreams of the enlargement of the church, the foreshadowing of the universal extension of the kingdom and the continued good work of the leaven in the three measures of meal, etc. It is hard to get the individual believer, brought up in these wrong conceptions, to see the true meaning; and often the true testimony given is rejected. Let us then carefully and prayerfully look into the chapter before us, and may our Lord give His blessing; and while the many may reject what is taught in these parables a few will receive light through the entrance of His Word, and all believers in these truths will be strengthened by our meditations.

Let us notice, first of all, two verses in this chapter; "Because to you it is given to know the mysteries of the kingdom of the heavens, but to them it is not given" (verse 11); "All these things Jesus spoke to the multitudes in parables, and without a parable He did not, speak to them, so that it might be fulfilled which was spoken through the prophets saying, I will open my mouth in parables; I will utter things hidden from the world's foundation": (verses 34-35). These verses then tell us what our Lord makes known in this chapter, namely *"the mysteries of the kingdom of the heavens"*—*"Things uttered, which were hidden from the world's foundation."*

3

In Genesis we read of one who is called "Zaphnath-paaneah" which, according to rabbinical interpretation, means "Revealer of secrets." He is Joseph, the Hebrew lad rejected by his brethren, that most perfect type of our Lord. After his rejection by his brethren, Joseph becomes the revealer of the secrets, and that through the wisdom of God.

Here in this chapter Christ appears as the rejected one, and now after the offer of the kingdom is rejected by the people of the kingdom, and He as king, is likewise rejected, He becomes the revealer of the secrets, to show what will take place after the kingdom has been rejected by Israel.

That He is the rejected one and the important witness He gives now is evident in the very opening verses. "And that same day Jesus went out from the house and sat down by the sea." Leaving the house means, He severed His relations with His people as we see at the close of the twelfth chapter. Taking His place by the sea, the sea typifying nations, shows that His testimony to be given now, the mysteries to be revealed have a different sphere; they are relative to the nations. "And great multitudes were gathered together to Him, so that going on board of a ship Himself, He sat down, and the whole crowd stood on the shore." He separated himself from the multitude, while in the first part of this Gospel He

moves in the midst of the multitudes, here He
takes His place alone. What a scene it must
have been. There on the seashore the multitudes, and He alone some ways from the shore
—He cannot be reached by *touch* now. All is
significant. Then when all eyes hang upon
His lips, He began to speak.

What He says is in parables, and without
parables He did not speak to them. He utters
seven parables. In no other Gospel do we find
them grouped together as here. Why is this?
The reason is obvious. This is the great dispensational Gospel. Here God's plan of the
ages is revealed as in no other Gospel.
The Holy Spirit in giving us this Gospel, the Genesis of the New Testament,
is not tied down to chronological order,
but He arranges everything to suit His sublime
purpose. After the kingdom was offered and
rejected, the Lord makes known what is to be
after His rejection, and during the time of His
absence. Therefore these parables, seven in
number, denoting completeness, are put right
in here.

Now the important question is when the
Lord says six times in these parables, "The
kingdom of the heavens is like" what does He
mean by the term "Kingdom of the heavens?"
That it can no longer mean the kingdom as it
is revealed in the Old Testament, as it is promised to Israel, and as He offered it to the peo-

ple, is evident. For in the first place, the offer was made and rejected. The preaching of Him and the messengers He sent out was, "The kingdom of the heavens is at hand, repent." Not a word do we hear of this in the thirteenth chapter, nor after this chapter. And in the second place, if our Lord had had the Old Testament kingdom promised to Israel in view, when He says here "The kingdom of the heavens is like," He could not have said that He uttered things hidden from the world's foundation, for the kingdom in the Old Testament is not a mystery, but clearly revealed.

Some say, and indeed the popular and almost universally accepted interpretation is—it is the church. The Lord begins now to teach about the church. So that if He says: "The kingdom of the heavens is like leaven, which a woman took and hid in three measures of meal, etc.," it is declared the church is meant, and the Gospel. The church is nowhere called the kingdom of the heavens. Oh, the sad and widespread confusion which exists on this topic. The Lord mentions the word church for the first time in the Gospel, in Matthew xvi, where He says that He *will build His church*. The church did not exist in the Old Testament, it was not known there at all; it was not in existence while the Lord walked on the earth, and *nowhere* does He refer to the church as the kingdom of the heavens, neither does the Holy Spirit speak of the church as the kingdom. He speaks of the church as the habitation of God, a house, a temple, the body of Christ and the Bride of Christ, but we repeat it, *never* as the kingdom of the heavens. All this modern application of the kingdom of the heavens to the church is foreign to the Word of God. It is the unscriptural theory of man.

But what does our Lord mean when He says "the kingdom of the heavens?" The answer is a very simple one. The kingdom on the one hand was rejected by Israel, but on the other hand, God gives His Word to the Gentiles, a fact indicated in the Old Testament prophetic Word.

The mercy and grace offered to Israel is to go forth to the Gentiles, the nations, while the King Himself is absent. This very fact is indicated in the first parable where the sower *went out,* which stands for the fact of His going forth into the field, which is the world. So that which is extended to the Gentiles and that in which the name of Christ is confessed is now the kingdom of the heavens, and of this development of what He the Lord from heaven brought and left in the earth, our Lord speaks in these parables. In one word "the kingdom of the heavens" in Matthew is equivalent with *"Christendom."* It includes the whole sphere of Christian profession saved

and unsaved, so-called Romanists and Protestants, all who. are naming the name of Christ.
Therefore the church is not the kingdom of
the heavens, though the church is in the kingdom of the heavens.

The Lord teaches in the seven parables how
matters will go in the earth while He is not
here, and what men will do with that which He
brought from heaven and left in the hands of
men.

Before we take up the parables separately
we must consider their general character. The
seven parables are first divided into four and
three. The first four He speaks before the multitudes. Then after He dismissed the crowds,
He went into the house and in the presence of
the disciples He utters the three last parables.
These three last ones, the treasure hid in the
field, the pearl of great price and the dragnet,
have a deeper spiritual meaning than the first.
The first two parables our Lord explains Himself to His disciples; the other five He leaves
unexplained.

They may also be divided in the following
way by twos:

1. The sower who went out to sow.

2. The enemy sowing tares, the spurious
seed.

These refer in part to the *beginning* of the
kingdom of the heavens in the hands of men,

however the conditions pictured here last to the end, the time of the harvest.

3. The parable of the mustard seed.

4. The parable of the leaven.

These foretell the external and internal development of the kingdom of the heavens; the progress is described and it is an unnatural and evil progress.

5. The parable of the treasure hid in the field.

6. The parable of the one pearl.

These stand for the two mysteries in the kingdom, God's earthly people hid in the field, the church the one pearl for which He has given all. First the pearl is taken, then the treasure is lifted in the field.

7. The parable of the dragnet.

It stands isolated, and refers to the end of the kingdom of the heavens in its mystery form.

Still another way of looking at them would be to compare them with the seven church messages in Rev. ii and iii. Here the Lord speaks again, and this speaking is from the glory. In the seven messages we learn the beginning, the progress and the end of this present Christian age. It is the history of Christendom, the kingdom of the heavens.

1. The parable of the sower—*Ephesus*. The apostolic age. The beginning with its failure —leaving the first love.

2. The parable of the evil seed—*Smyrna,* meaning bitterness. The enemy revealed.

3. The parable of the mustard seed—*Pergamos*—meaning high tower or married. The professing church becomes big, a state institution under Constantine the Great. The big tree and the unclean birds (nations) find shelter there.

4. The parable of the leaven—*Thyatira.* This is Rome and her abomination. The woman Jezebel, the harlot, corresponds to the woman in the parable of the leaven.

5. The parable of the treasure hid—*Sardis* —the reformation age—having a name to live, but being dead and a remnant there. Israel, dead but belonging to Him who has purchased the field.

6. The parable of the Pearl—*Philadelphia.* The church, the *one* pearl. The one body of Christ and the removal of the church to be with Him.

7. The parable of the dragnet—*Laodicea*— Judgment. I will spue thee out of my mouth. We do not claim to teach all this in detail. That would take many pages, but we give these that each reader has hints in what way to search.

We add but one more fact to these introductory remarks for the study of the different parables. The key for their right interpretation is in themselves as well as in the scriptures. The

sower in the first parable and in the second is
the Son of Man. What He sows is the wheat,
that which stands throughout the scriptures for
purity, for Christ himself. The Word He is
Himself and the corn of wheat; the good seed
are the sons of the kingdom. The field is the
world. The enemy is the Devil. The man in
the sixth parable who buys the field (the
world) is the same Son of Man and the merchantman who sells all He has to purchase the
one pearl He desires is the same person as the
Sower. It is nonsense to make out of the mer-
chantmen and out of the man who buys the
field the sinner. That would mean that the
sinner has something to give. He has not.
And the field, meaning the world, it would
mean the sinner is to buy the world.

The three measures of meal of course come
from the wheat, they *always stand* for that
which is good. Leaven, however, *never* means
anything good, but it always stands for evil.
The closer study of these parables, which we
now take up will bring out all this more fully.

· II.

After having studied this important chapter
in a general way, we shall now look at the
seven parables separately and to learn from

them the development of the Kingdom of the Heavens in its mystery form. Throughout our study the dispensational aspect of the parables is to be kept strongly in the foreground, for it is dispensational truth which is taught here.

The first parable is the well-known one of the sower. "And he spoke to them many things in parables, saying, Behold the sower went out to sow." Two things attract our attention in this opening sentence of the parable. We notice first that our Lord speaks of *the* sower, not of *a* sower, and when He expounds the parable later to His disciples He does not tell them who this sower is, but He only speaks of what happens to the seed He sowed. The second thing we mention is that the sower went *out*.

The personality of the sower is not difficult to clear up, for in explaining the second parable our Lord says: "He that soweth the good seed is the Son of Man." Our Lord Himself is the Sower. He came with the precious seed, the fine wheat, and of course He Himself is the corn of wheat. The seed He sows can only bring forth as it falls upon good ground, and in the ground it dies, and out of death comes the fruit. All this is indicated here. We would, however, take this parable in the first sense to apply to the days of our Lord in the earth. In a wider sense it must be taken as typical of the entire age, in which He is absent

from the earth. The sowing He began continues still, and the result of the sowing is likewise the same.

And what is the significance that it is written
that the sower went *out* to sow? It shows the
beginning of something new; a new work
which the Lord now takes up. Israel had failed
to yield fruit. Israel was the vineyard of Isaiah
v. "He fenced it in, and gathered out the
stones thereof, and planted it with the choicest
vines, and built a tower in the midst of it, and
also made a wine press therein; and He looked
that it should bring forth grapes, and it brought
forth wild grapes . . . and now go to; I
will tell you what I will do to my vineyard: I
will take away the hedge thereof, and it shall
be eaten up; and break down the wall thereof,
and it shall be trodden down." (Is. v:2-7.)
Israel is the fig tree of the parable; the Lord
came and found no fruit. The vineyard is laid
waste and the fig tree stands barren. It is true,
it will not be always so. The vine and the fig
tree will bring fruit at last, but in the mean-
time, while Israel is unfruitful, the sower has
gone out to sow. Where has he gone? Where
does the sower generally deposit the seed? In
the field? What is the field? The divine in-
terpreter gives us the answer. "The field is
the world." So we have here the fact established that after Israel failed the Word is to
go forth into the wide world, "beginning in

Jerusalem unto Samaria and the uttermost
parts of the earth."

The question comes at once, what will be the
result? Will all the world receive it and every
part of the entire field be cultivated? Will
the whole field be reached by the seed and
the seed spring up and bear an abundant harvest? Will not a single grain be lost? The
parable has this very thought as its centre,
What becomes of the seed?

What we learn from the parable is far from
teaching us the optimistic dream of Christendom of world conversion, so often founded
upon a wrong application of these parables.
The parable proves that it will not be a universal acceptance of the Word which we can
look for in this age; only the fourth part of
the seed sown brings forth fruit, and there is
again a marked difference in the quantity of
fruit in that fourth part. Our Lord then im-
presses here in this simple parable the fact,
which later the Holy Spirit repeats, the age in
which He is absent and in which His Word
is preached and His grace is offered, that
Word will be in greater part rejected, and
only a fourth part yields the fruit; the rest is
failure.

It is very significant that we meet this important dispensational fact at the very thresh-
old of Matthew xiii. Alas; it has not been
believed by the great mass of professing Chris-

tians. To speak of failure in this age and deny a soon coming world conversion is frowned upon as a miserable, unbelieving pessimism. One is sometimes even accused of disbelieving the power of the Holy Spirit to convert the whole world, as if the Holy Spirit had been sent down from heaven for world conversion.

But we shall now read what came from the lips of our Lord in this parable.

"Behold the sower went out to sow; and as he sowed, some grains fell along the way, and the birds came and devoured them; and others fell upon the rocky places where they had not much earth, and immediately they sprang up out of the ground, because of not having any depth of earth, but when the sun rose they were burned up, and because of not having any root were dried up; and others fell upon the thorns, and the thorns grew up and choked them; and others fell upon the good ground, and produced fruit, one a hundred, one sixty, and one thirty. He that has ears let him hear" (verses 5-9). We need not to guess the meaning of this parable, for the Lord Himself tells His disciples what He meant by the birds and the rocky place and the thorns. And so we shall take His own explanation with such comments as may be helpful for a fuller understanding.

"The disciples came up to Him and said, Why speakest thou to them in parables?" This

question came at once after He had finished
this first parable. They had never heard a
parable from His lips. What He had spoken
before to the people and their leaders had been
in simple words, easily to be understood by
every one, and now for the first time He spoke
something which they could not comprehend.
It was veiled. The answer which our Lord
gives is of great solemnity, as it announces the
judgment upon Israel.

"And He answering said to them, Because
to you it is given to know the mysteries of the
Kingdom of the Heavens, but to them it is not
given." The disciples, representing believers,
were to understand the mysteries coming in
now while the nation who had refused the
light would be in darkness. "For whosoever
has, to him shall be given, and he shall be
caused to be in abundance. But he who has
not, even what he has shall be taken away from
him." The disciples had received the Lord
and He gave them more, while Israel had not,
they rejected Christ and so what they had
still as His earthly people was to be taken
away from them. But this two-edged sword
cuts in another way. The principle our Lord
here utters is still active. The true believers
composing the church have, and by and by
we shall be caused to be in abundance, while
an apostate Christendom which has not shall
lose even what it boasts to have.

"For this cause," our Lord continues, "I speak to them in parables, because seeing they do not see, and hearing they do not hear nor understand; and in them is filled up the prophecy of Esaias, which says, Hearing ye shall hear and shall not understand, and beholding ye shall behold and not see; for the heart of this people has grown fat, and they have heard heavily with their ears, and they have closed their eyes as asleep, lest they should see with the eyes, and hear with the ears, and understand with the heart, and should be converted, and I should heal them." This passage is a quotation from Isaiah vi:9-10. · Isaiah saw in a vision Jehovah sitting upon a throne, and He spoke these words to the prophet. If we turn to the xii. chapter in the Gospel of John we read the same words quoted again, and there is the significant addition, "These things said Esaias, when He saw His glory, and spoke of Him" (John xii:40). The Jehovah Isaiah saw upon His throne was our Lord Jesus Christ. Once more do we read the same words brought to remembrance by the Holy Spirit. In the last chapter of Acts, when Israel's apostasy and unbelief is fully established, Paul speaks them to the assembled Jews and adds, "Be it known therefore unto you that the salvation of God is sent unto the Gentiles and they will hear."

And now after our Lord declares them

blessed on account of what they see and hear, He explains the parable Himself.

"Ye, therefore, hear the parable of the sower. From every one who hears the word of the Kingdom and does not understand it, the wicked one comes and catches away what was sown in his heart; this is he that is sown at the wayside" (v. 18-19).

How easy is it then understood. The wayside is hard and trodden down by feet, there the seed fell and birds were ready to snatch it up and devour it.

A hearer or a class of hearers is given here who do not understand the Word. But is it the question of mental capacity of an intellectual understanding? Certainly not The Lord says the word was "sown in the heart·" it had directed itself to the conscience and could either be accepted or rejected. But the heart would not have it and turned against it· "and does not understand it," means "he *would* not understand or receive it." No sooner is this the case and the seed has fallen upon such a ground, a hard heart like the wayside, then the birds come and devour the seed. The birds represent the wicked one. He is present with his agencies and busy to take up whatever was given. Once more do we read in this chapter of birds; it is in the third parable, that of the mustard seed. The birds there mean nothing good but that which is evil, as in the first parable.

"But he that is sown on the rocky places—this is he that hears the Word and immediately receives it with joy, but has no root in himself, but is for a time only; and when tribulation happens on account of the Word, he is immediately offended" (vv. 20-21).

The rocky ground is lightly covered with earth. There is a sudden springing up, an enthusiastic reception one might say, which pushes itself along. But the sun rises higher, the heat is felt, and there is no resistance, no life to combat these conditions; the delicate thing drops over and is burned up. It had no roots. This little earth on top of the rock may well represent the natural heart of man as the way trodden by men represents it. Only here is the brightest side of the flesh, if one can speak of it in such a way. But behind that little earth is the solid rock, which no plow has broken and in which no life is present. How large is this class? It is the great class of professing Christians. They are covering over this old, desperately wicked heart with a little earth. They put on the form of Godliness, while they know nothing of its power. There is also a great deal of enthusiasm, a springing up of the seed; it looks almost as if there is to be a great result—but alas! there is only the name to live, but death is behind it.

"When the sun rose they were burned up."
May we not apply this word also dispensation-
ally? The rocky ground sowers will flourish,
and they flourish and increase now with their
empty profession and their enthusiastic show
of religiousness and world improvement. But
the sun will rise, tribulation will come. The
great tribulation and the judgments, which
precede the rising of the Sun of Righteousness
will burn them up and sweep them away.

"And he that is sown among the thorns,
this is he who hears the Word, and the anx-
ious care of this life and the deceit of riches
choke the Word and he becomes unfruitful"
(verse 22).

This is so plain that it needs hardly any
comment at all. "The deceit of riches" hinder
the growth of the Word. It becomes choked
and there is no fruit. How true this is of
the present day we all know. The world, the
pleasures of the earth, cares and anxiety in
getting as much as possible of these phantom
things here seems to control more and more
the outwardly professing masses. All that is
of God becomes choked.

Thus we see in these three classes, in which
the seed perishes and brings no fruit, the Devil,
the Flesh and the World represented. The
Devil snatches up and devours, the Flesh attempts and fails, the World surrounds and
chokes. And yet how much else might be said

in connection with these three classes! No
human being could have spoken such a simple
parable with such a deep and far-reaching
meaning. The Revealer of Secrets speaks,
who knows the hidden things.

"But he that is sown upon the good ground,
this is he who hears and understands the Word,
who bears fruit also and produces one a hundred, one sixty, and one thirty" (verse 23).
Hearing, understanding, which is in faith and
through faith, fruitbearing and producing, this
is the process of the seed in the good ground,
a receptive heart prepared by the Grace of
God.

III.

We come now to the second parable, in
which we find the Kingdom of the heavens
mentioned. It was not mentioned in connection with the first parable of the sower. "Another parable set He before them, saying,
The Kingdom of the heavens has become like
a man sowing good seed in his field; but while
men slept his enemy came and sowed darnel
amongst the wheat and went away. But when
the blade shot up and produced fruit then ap-
peared the darnel also. And the bondmen of
the householder came up and said to him. Sir,
hast thou not sown good seed in thy field?

Whence then has it darnel? And he said to them, A man that is an enemy has done this. And the bondmen said to him, Wilt thou then that we go and gather it up? But he said, No; lest in gathering the darnel ye should root up the wheat with it. Suffer both to grow together unto the harvest, and in time of the harvest I will say to the harvestmen, Gather first the darnel, and bind it into bundles to burn it; but the wheat bring together into my granary" (verses 24-30). Again we are not left to seek for an interpretation. After he had spoken two other parables we read that our Lord in answer to His disciples' question tells them what He meant by the parable. To this perfect interpretation by the divine speaker we have to turn to find the correct and far reaching meaning of this second parable. "Then, having dismissed the crowds, He went into the house; and His disciples came to Him, saying, Expound to us the parable of the darnel of the field. But He answering said, He that sows the good seed is the Son of Man, and the field is the world and the good seed these are the Sons of the Kingdom, but the darnel are the sons of the evil one; and the enemy who has sowed it is the devil, and the harvest is the completion of the age, and the harvestmen are angels" (verses 36-39).

The connection with the first parable is clear. The same sower is in the beginning of the parable before us, and the seed is deposited in the field, which is the world. But our Lord says, "the good seed, these are the Sons of the Kingdom." This can mean only one thing, namely, that the good seed sown and fallen into a good ground, as we saw in the first parable, brings forth fruit, and the Word of the Kingdom produces the Sons of the Kingdom. Like begets like; the fruit is according to the seed. However, the leading thought in this parable is the enemy and his evil work. It is a work of spite, as it is yet quite often practiced in oriental countries. The enemy watches till his hated neighbor has deposited his seed into the field, then he goes to work during the night, while men sleep, and begins to sow the bad seed of some weed. Not till the seed springs up and grows does the unsuspecting victim see the work of the enemy. The enemy, our Lord says, is the devil. As from the Word of the Kingdom the Sons of the Kingdom spring forth, so from the evil seed sown by the devil come the sons of the evil one.

It is important to notice the *time* when the enemy did this and the *manner* in which he attempts to counteract the work of the Sower, the Son of Man.

In regard to the time, we have two facts to consider. The first is: It was immediately after the Sower had deposited the good seed;

and the second fact: It was "while men slept."
No sooner had our Lord brought the truth,
and the Holy Spirit had been given, than the
enemy began its work. In the days of the
Apostle Paul the work which the enemy had
done became manifest, and the evil seed, which
at the end of this age is full grown, is easily
seen springing up in the beginning of the age.
The mystery of iniquity began its work then,
and continues throughout the age till the end
is reached, when it is fully developed.

It was while men slept that the enemy did it.
Not the Sower slept, He neither sleeps nor
slumbers, but the men slept. Such an un-
watchful condition soon developed in the beginning of the age. The first love was soon
given up, and then the enemy did his work.

The manner was by putting a counterfeit
seed in the field. The darnel looks in its seed
like the wheat. When it springs up it cannot
be distinguished from the wheat, yet it is a
poisonous weed. The darnel represents the
lie as it is put into the field by the devil. It
is evil doctrine, a counterfeit of the faith once
and for all delivered unto the saints. The denial of the Deity of our Lord, the denial of the
resurrection and the inspiration of the Bible
belong to this darnel seed, which made itself
felt in the very beginning of this Christian age.

In a certain sense this process still continues.
Whenever the truth is proclaimed and the

Word taught, it does not take long before the enemy comes and brings the counterfeit when "men sleep." Another strong lesson we learn from this parable is the character of this entire age. It is evil. Satan is the god of this age till the end of the age comes. The mixed condition of good seed and darnel seed, Sons of the Kingdom and sons of the evil one prevails to the very end. The servants of the bondmen were willing to root out the darnel but were not permitted to do so. It is an idle dream, which many hope to realize, to reform the world, to gather out obnoxious evils, to banish drunkenness and immorality, to purify the state and politics. Such efforts are nowhere taught in the Word of God. Men, under Christian profession, take such work upon themselves, and they little know how they sin and dishonor Christ with it. No, error and its fruits will continue to grow alongside the good seed and its precious fruit till the time of the harvest. Before we follow the thought of the harvest we turn our attention to still another matter in connection with the first part of this parable.

A vital error has been committed in regard to the place where the wheat and the darnel grow together. It has been said to us "we cannot have a pure church, or assembly, for the Lord Himself has said that the evil will always be with us and that we are not to put

them out who are the sons of the evil one."
This was said and is said on the supposition
that our Lord speaks of the Church. However, this is not the case. The church, the
assembly, is not before Him at all. As we
have said before the Kingdom of the heavens
is not the Church. When it comes to the revelation concerning the Church we hear our
Lord say that evil is not to be tolerated in the
assembly. "If thy brother sin against thee go,
reprove him between thee and him alone. If
he hear thee, thou hast gained thy brother.
But if he do not hear, take with thee one or
two besides that every matter may stand upon
the word of two witnesses or of three. But
if he will not listen to them, tell it to the assembly; and if also he will not listen to the
assembly, let him be to thee as one of the
nations and a taxgatherer" (Chap. xviii:15-
17). This is the way evil is to be treated in
the assembly or, as we generally say, Church.
In the epistles we find numerous exhortations
that evil doctrine and an evil walk contrary to
the Gospel is not to be tolerated in an assembly. The assembly is to judge evil. It is *not*
said of the Church "let them grow together."

The field is not the Church, but the world,
and it is in the world that this takes place; in
been sown, in the entire sphere of professing
that part of the field where the good seed has
Christendom.

The harvest is the completion of the age.
Our authorized version has it "world." This
has misled many readers of the Word. The
end of this world is a good ways off yet. The
age in which we live is drawing rapidly
to a close. What will take place then?
Our Lord says, "As then the darnel is gathered and is burned in the fire, thus it shall be
in the completion of the age. The Son of
Man shall send His angels and they shall
gather out of His Kingdom all offences, and
those that practice lawlessness, and they shall
cast them into the furnace of fire; there shall
be the weeping and gnashing of teeth. Then
the righteous shall shine forth as the sun in
the Kingdom of their father. He that hath
ears let him hear" (verses 40-43). Before in
the parable our Lord said: "I will say to the
harvestmen, Gather first the darnel, and bind
it into bundles to burn it; but the wheat bring
together into my granary."

The completion of the age is the same as in
Matthew xxiv, when the disciples asked for
the signs of His coming and the completion of
the age. The ending of the age will be Jewish;
Jewish history resumed in the events which
fall into the last week of Daniel, the seventieth
week. Of this ending the Lord speaks. The
angels will then be the harvestmen. It corresponds to what we read in Rev. xiv:14-20.
"And I looked and behold a white cloud, and

upon the cloud one sat like unto the Son of
Man, having upon His head a golden crown,
and in His hand a sharp sickle. And another
angel came out of the temple, crying with a
loud voice to him that sat on the cloud. Thrust
in thy sickle and reap; for the time is come
for thee to reap, for the harvest of the earth
is ripe."

Some who teach that unscriptural theory.
that the church will remain in the earth to the
very end of the age and pass through the great
tribulation, have used this parable to support
their views. We repeat the parable has nothing to do with the Church. When our Lord
speaks of the bundling up of the darnel and
the gathering of the wheat into the granary,
He did not teach that the wheat is the Church
or represents the Church, and that the gathering in of the Church is to be His last act in
this age. The wheat, of course, is the good
seed, the good seed are the Sons of the Kingdom. That all true believers are the good
seed and as such Sons of the Kingdom none
would doubt. Yet, after the Church is removed from the earth, before the completion
of the age, as foretold in prophecy, begins,
there will still be wheat in the earth. There
will still be sowing. Indeed it will then be
"the Word of the Kingdom" which is preached.
The Gospel of the Kingdom will be proclaimed
during that end and the seed will spring up.

A great multitude will come out of that great tribulation having washed their robes in the blood of the Lamb. This multitude will be gathered in the time when the darnel are being bundled up, preparatory to the visible manifestation of the Lord. The wheat, these Sons of the Kingdom, will be gathered into His granary, kept and preserved for the Kingdom to be established in the earth. "Then the righteous shall shine forth as the sun in the Kingdom of their Father." This reminds us very strongly of the language of Matthew xxv:34. "Come ye blessed of My Father, inherit the Kingdom prepared for you from the foundation of the World." These words are addressed *not* to the church, but to that multitude come out of all nations (Rev. vii) and the Kingdom is not the heavenly glory but the *earthly* Kingdom. The Church, her heavenly calling and destination, we repeat again, is *not* in view at all in this second parable.

Let us hold fast the three great facts the parable teaches. These are, as we have seen, the following:

1. The enemy, the devil, began his work in the beginning of the age.

2. The age is mixed, good and evil grows together. This condition cannot be changed throughout the age.

3. The mixed condition will cease with the

completion of the age. The Sons of the Kingdom will inherit the Kingdom. The darnel after being bundled up are burned with fire.

IV.

The next two parables our Lord spake to reveal still more of the mysteries of the kingdom of the heavens are the parables of the mustard seed and of the leaven. They belong together. We shall learn in the exposition of these two parables, how the popular interpretation of them through the leading commentators of Christendom has turned everything upside down. The fact is, precisely the opposite our Lord meant is being taught by teachers in evangelical Christendom. The fault of this erroneous interpretation springs from the great fundamental error that the Lord has the church in view when He speaks of the kingdom of the heavens, and that the church is that kingdom. Therefore it is taken for granted by this false exposition that when the Lord now speaks of a grain of mustard seed, which becomes a great tree and which gives shelter to the birds, that this is a prophecy relating to the expansion of the church. The leaven is therefore made to mean the gospel with its leavening power. All this is *radically* wrong.

We turn to the parable of the grain of mustard seed first.

"Another parable set He before them, saying, The kingdom of the heavens is like a grain of mustard seed which a man took and sowed in his field, which is less indeed than all seeds, but when it is grown is greater than herbs, and becomes a tree, so that the birds of heaven come and roost in its branches" (verses 31-32).

Here we have the outward development of the kingdom of the heavens as it grows and expands, in an unnatural way, and becomes the roosting place of the birds of heaven. As indicated above, the almost universal comment on this mustard seed and its miraculous growth, as it is termed, is that it fully declares the expansion of the church, and the birds of heaven are interpreted as meaning peoples and nations, who find shelter in the church. Growing and still growing, the mustard tree reaches over the entire earth, its branches spread out wider and wider, and soon (so they tell us) the tree will have covered the earth as the waters cover the deep. It is also a common occurrence that some denominational leader—a bishop or an elder—claims the parable for his denomination and illustrates with it the phenomenal growth of the sect to which he belongs, or claims a great future of success. Again, the history of the "church" is resorted to for the sake of showing the fulfilment of this parable and the statistics of Christendom, so many millions of Protestants (including all the infidels, unsaved masses of Germany, England, and every other "evangelical" country) now, so many more than fifty years ago, etc.

Now, if the Lord had meant His church by this mustard seed, which becomes a tree and the roosting place of birds, if it is really the church, which is His body, then this parable would be in flagrant contradiction with what He and the Holy Spirit teach elsewhere concerning the church in the earth, the mission and the future of the church. The greatest clash of teaching would be the result.

For instance, in His prayer our Lord says concerning His own, those who are one as the Father and Son are one: "They are not of the world, as I am not of the world" (John xvii: 14). The church then, composed of all believers, is not of the world as He is not of the world. The church is from above, as every believer has a life which is from above; but for a little while the church is *in* the world, and in a little while the church will be above, where He is the glorified Head of His body. The mustard seed springing up in the field (do not forget the field is the *world*), rooting deeper and deeper in the earth and expanding in this unnatural way affording room for birds, is the picture of something entirely different. It shows us a system which is rooted in the earth and which aims at greatness in the world, expansion over the earth. The Lord never meant His church to be rooted and grounded in the field, the world. He never called the church to assume such proportions and become an abnormal growth in the earth. Whatever is spoken of Christ is spoken of the church. Suffering and glory, lowliness followed by exaltation, is the way Christ went; it is the way ordained for the church. She is to be lowly, now suffering with Him, rejected and disowned by the world as He was, never to reign and rule now, but patiently waiting with Him for the moment when He is manifested and *then* to share His Throne and His Glory. The calling and destiny of the church is heavenly. Her mission is to shine out Himself and testify of His grace, but never to control and overspread the world. The epistles addressed to the church make this sufficiently clear.

But if the mustard seed and its growth does not mean the *church*, what does it mean? It means the Kingdom of the heavens, and this is, as we have seen before, professing Christendom. At once the parable becomes illuminated with light. Looked upon in this light, in full harmony with all the Lord teaches in this chapter, all is easily understood. The little mustard seed, which was not destined to be a tree but only a shrub, easily taken out of the garden where it had been planted, develops against its nature into a tree. That which came from Him, the Son of Man, the Sower, develops, committed into the hands of men, into an unnatural thing—one might say, a monstrosity—for such a mustard *tree* is. This unnatural thing, this monstrosity, is professing Christendom as a system of the world, professing Christ, without possessing Him and His Spirit.

Here we have to call attention to the third message to the churches in Revelation, the second chapter. That is the message to Pergamos, typifying the age of the history of Christendom, beginning with Constantine the Great in the fourth century. The professing church was made a state church. The mustard seed *suddenly* became the tree, and ever since the professing church has delighted in looking upon herself as a big expanding tree. But notice the perfect agreement—the third parable and the third church message.

The birds which roost in that tree would have to mean, if the parable applies to the church, converted sinners. Do birds ever represent clean persons? We need not go outside of the chapter to answer this. The birds which fell upon the seed which had fallen by the wayside were instruments of Satan. Birds of heaven, or fowls, never mean anything good in Scripture. Abraham stood in the midst of the pieces of the sacrifices and drove away the fowls which were ready to fall upon the pieces (Gen. xv). The animals divided there represent Christ and the fowls nothing good. Birds in this parable mean unsaved, unconverted people and nations who flock for selfish motives to the tree, the outward form of Christendom, and find shelter there. But they defile the tree.

At last the tree will be full grown. Of the full grown tree it is said, "Great Babylon has become the habitation (roosting place) of demons, and a hold of every unclean spirit, and a hold of every *unclean and hated bird*" (Rev. xviii :2).

But let us not forget there is a tree which is to grow up and spread its branches, taking sap out of the root, over the whole earth. This tree is Israel—the good olive tree with its indestructible root. Some of the branches are now broken off and lie upon the ground. Romans xi, however, assures us that God is able to graft them in again. Yet before this olive tree with its holy root, this olive tree with its long promised future, the covenant made with an oath, stands highminded, boasting Christendom, boasting itself against the branches and claiming to be the tree to overspread the earth and thus attending to Israel's

earthly calling. Alas! the warning is cast
into the winds, "if God spared not the natural
branches take heed lest He spare not thee."
What a fall it will be when at last that tree,
the monstrous tree,' falls and is destroyed for-
ever root and all!

V.

But we must now turn our attention to the
next parable, the parable of the leaven. "He
spoke another parable to them: The kingdom
of the heavens is like leaven, which a woman
took and hid in three measures of meal until
it had been all leavened" (verse 33). It is,
perhaps, unnecessary to state the universal explanation of the parable of the leaven. All
the leading commentators of the Bible have
accepted it, and it is taught throughout Christendom. However, we must refer to it briefly.
The leaven is taken to mean the Gospel and
its power. The woman represents the church.
The woman takes the leaven and puts it into
three measures of meal, which, according to
this general exegesis, represents humanity, the
entire human family. Here the leaven does,
in a hidden manner, its work in an assimilating
process in penetrating the whole mass of humanity.*

That the parable *could* mean anything but

*Thus writes P. Lange, often called "the Prince
among Commentators." "The woman is an apt figure

that, which we have briefly outlined, seems to
the great majority of teachers and preachers
of Christendom next to an impossible thing.
It is such a generally accepted view that but
few can tear themselves loose from it, and
see the true teaching our Lord gives in this
fourth parable. One hears so continually
statements about the Gospel leaven and prayer
that the "good" leaven may do its work, etc.,
that another explanation of this parable puts
one at odds with the bulk of Christian believers. Indeed, this little parable contained in this
little verse is apt to revolutionize the concep-
tion of many truths revealed in the Word of
God. If we then approach this parable with a
candid mind, laying aside any prejudice and
preconceived ideas and are willing to know
and follow the truth at any cost, we shall certainly find the truth and with it great joy and
peace. If it revolutionizes our views it will
only put us *right*, for whosoever follows the
accepted teachings of men is generally not
right.

---

of the church. Leaven, a substance kindred, yet
quite opposed to meal, having the power of trans-
forming and preserving it, and converting it into
bread, thus representing the divine in its relation to,
and influence upon, our natural life. One of the
main points of the parable is the hiding or the mix-
ing of the leaven in the three measures of meal.
This refers to the great visible church, in which the
living Gospel seems, as it were, hidden and lost."

If then the leaven means the Gospel, and the woman the church, and the three measures of meal humanity, the Lord would teach that the Gospel, through the instrumentality of the church, is to permeate humanity, and that the world is to be converted by the assimilating power of the Gospel in penetrating the whole mass of humanity. Such, of course, *is* the belief, the unscriptural belief, of Christendom. But if the Lord teaches any such doctrine in this parable He manifestly contradicts Himself, a thing impossible with Him, who is infallible. We have seen in the second parable that the wheat and the tares grow together until the time of the harvest. This *excludes* the thought of world conversion in this age. This age, as we have seen, is a mixed one, and these conditions prevail to the end of it. If our Lord meant the leaven to permeate the whole lump of humanity then He teaches something entirely different from what He taught in the second parable.

But let us turn our attention to the word "leaven." We should not forget that our Lord as the teacher, as Nicodemus called Him, come from God, was according to the flesh the Son of David and the Son of Abraham. These to whom He speaks were Jews. Now the hearers of the parable certainly understood what was meant by leaven. No Jew would ever dream that leaven used in illus-

trating some power of process, could stand
for something good. Leaven with the Jews
means always evil. It was excluded from
every offering of the Lord made by fire. Con-
scientiously the orthodox Jew searches his
dwelling before keeping the feast of the un-
leavened bread, if perhaps somewhere a mor-
sel of bread with some leaven may be hid.
He purges out the leaven.

The word leaven, however, is not used here
exclusively. We find it a number of times in
the New Testament; the question is for what
does it stand in the other passages?

Three times our Lord uses the word leaven
besides here in the parable. He speaks of the
leaven of the Pharisees, the leaven of the Sadducees and the leaven of Herod. (Matt.
xvi:12; Mark viii:15.) Does he mean some
good quality of the Pharisees and Sadducees
when He mentions leaven in connection with
them? Certainly not, He cautions His disciples to beware of that leaven. He terms the
hypocrisy of the ritualistic Pharisee, leaven,
and the rationalism of the Sadducees and
worldliness of Herod is leaven. The Holy
Spirit furthermore uses the word leaven only
in an evil sense (1 Cor. v:6; Gal. v:9). It is
then evident in Scripture language leaven
never means anything good, *always* stands for
evil and corruption. It is impossible that it
should mean only *once* something good, and

that the Lord without any further comment, should use it here as a type of the gospel.

But let us turn to the question of the three measures of meal. What do they represent? The faulty but accepted teaching is, that the Lord means corrupted humanity by it. However, this is as impossible as it is for leaven to be something good. Where does the meal come from? Surely any child can answer this, the meal comes from the *wheat*. Tares, the type of evil, corruption, never yield fine, wholesome meal. Meal is the product of the good seed only. Good, nutritious and pure as it is, it can *never* represent the unregenerated mass of humanity. But we have still greater evidence. Three measures of meal (an ephah) stand in type for Christ, the corn of wheat and the bread of life. When Abraham comforted the Lord (Genesis xviii) it was by three measures of meal and a calf. Both are typical of Christ, His Person and His Work. He is good, pure, holy, undefiled, as well as that which He has given, His Word. It is therefore all folly to twist Scripture language around, and make the three measures of meal mean corruption, when it always denotes purity.

Again, if the Gospel is leaven, and this leaven is to pervade the whole mass of humanity, we have an additional contradiction. Does the Gospel really work like leaven? How

does leaven work? It is put into meal and then
it works by itself. That is all. Simply put it
there, leave it alone, it is bound to leaven the
whole lump. But this is *not* the way the Gospel works the power of God unto salvation.

Conceding that it is true, the Gospel is leaven
and is to pervade the whole lump, then we can
readily say the "Gospel leaven" is the biggest
failure which has ever been put out. There is
no nation, nor even a town or hamlet which
has ever been successfully "leavened" by the
Gospel.

The process is then a failure, the Gospel
does not accomplish the leavening of the
lump. It has not done it in 1900 years. The
inference which comes next is, that in giving
such a prophecy the speaker, our Lord, was
mistaken.

We have now torn down the false explanation of the parable, and laid the foundation
upon which we can easily build and grasp the
true meaning of the parable.

Leaven is error, evil, corruption The good
pure meal stands for truth, for Christ and his
Word. The leaven corrupts the meal, it
changes that which is good, and attacks in a
hidden way its purity, till it has pervaded the
whole mass. The Lord teaches in the parable
how evil doctrine will corrupt the fine meal,
the doctrine of Christ. It follows the parable
of the mustard seed. First the professing

church was lifted up into prominence, and the next step was the woman who put leaven into the three measures of meal. Pergamos, the period of church history, in which the professing church is married (the meaning of Pergamos) to the state and the world, is followed by the fourth period, that of Thyatira. This fourth message corresponds to the parable of the woman and the leaven. A woman, the woman Jezebel, is mentioned in Revelation ii. No doubt she stands for Rome. The woman in the parable represents the same, the apostate church, the mother of harlots and abominations of the earth. She has with her evil doctrine, the leaven, corrupted the fine meal, the doctrine of Christ. And now this leaven works in professing Christendom. It has not yet fully pervaded all, the whole is not yet leavened. The true believers, the church, still on the earth, are a hindrance to the full leavening process of evil. But the church will be removed from the earth, then the whole lump will be leavened. The fire alone can arrest the leaven in its work. The fire will make an end of the leaven. This explanation is the only correct one, for it agrees perfectly not only with the teaching of our Lord in the previous parables, but with Scripture as a whole. The evil conditions in which the kingdom of the heavens gets in the hands of men, during the absence of the Lord, is here

fully declared. Christendom, Rome, the
mother of harlots, and the daughters, is evidence enough and proof how the Revealer of
Secrets revealed things to come.

All these parables show the growth of *evil*,
and are prophecies extending over the entire
age in which we live. May we bow before
the Word and follow the Word and its clear
teachings, the oracles of God, rather than the
"voice of the church" or "the doctrines of
men."

VI.

After our Lord dismissed the multitudes, He
went into the house and here, in answer to
the request of the disciples, He expounded the
second parable. It was given to them, as it
is given to us, to know the mysteries of the
kingdom. We have looked at this divine interpretation before, and so we can at once pro-
ceed with the three parables which follow and
which our Lord speaks to His disciples in the
house. Two of these, the parable of the treasure hid in the field and the parable of the one
pearl of great price, belong together. After
these the Lord concludes His teaching on the
mysteries with the parable of the dragnet.

"The kingdom of the heavens is like a treasure hid in the field, which a man having found

has hid, and for the joy of it goes and sells all whatever he has, and buys that field. Again the kingdom of the heavens is like a merchantman seeking beautiful pearls; and having found one pearl of great value, he went and sold all whatever he had and bought it" (verses 44-46). That these two parables are closely connected is seen by their similarity. In both a man is mentioned, and he sells in either one all he has to obtain what he esteems precious. In the first, he finds a treasure in the field and hides it there, while he buys the field to possess the treasure. In the second, he sells all to obtain one pearl of great value. There is, of course, a difference, likewise. The treasure is in the field; it is deposited there. The field is bought, and with it the treasure. The one pearl comes out of the sea; its value is greater than treasure in the field, of which it is not said that it has a great value. Again, a treasure may be increased or decreased, there may be taken away from it or added to it; the one pearl, however, is complete, its value and beauty are fixed.

As we turn to the interpretation of these parables, we are obliged to follow the same course which we followed with the preceding parables. We have to set aside the commonly accepted view. We have to show once more that the almost universal exposition and application of the parables by evangelical Chris-

tendom is wrong, unscriptural and conflicting
with other parts of God's Word. We shall
have to use the sharp knife again, to lay bare
the errors of the teachings taken from the
treasure in the field and the one pearl. Only
in this way can we get at the root of the matter, and see the true meaning and understand
the mysteries of the kingdom.

Perhaps the best way to mention the erroneous interpretation is to quote the father of
Protestantism, Martin Luther. His comment
on these two parables is about the best ex-
pression of the accepted theories, what our
Lord meant with the treasure and the pearl.
Luther said:

The parable of the treasure means, that we vainly
seek the kingdom of God by our works and exertion,
or the works of the law. For we are not born of
the blood, nor of the will of the flesh, nor of the
will of man. The Jews had the field, but did not
see the treasure in it. But the Gentiles bought the
field with the treasure; that is the *law with Christ*.
. . . . . The hidden treasure *is the Gospel*,
which gives us grace and righteousness without our
merit. Therefore when one finds it, it causes joy;
that is a good, cheerful conscience, which cannot be
secured by any good works.

The parable of the pearl is almost of the same
import as the preceding one, except that the former
speaks of the finding and this of the seeking. Therefore he speaks here of a growing faith, and signifies
therewith that the pearl was not unknown, but that
it had been heard of, as being of great price. Here
the merchantman is intent only, that he may possess

the one pearl. For this is also the nature of the Christian life, that he who has begun it imagines he has nothing, but he reaches out for it, and constantly presses onward, that he may obtain it.*

This mode of interpretation has been strictly followed by commentators. H. A. W. Meyer, a leading expositor of the New Testament, declares "the kingdom, the most valuable possession, must be taken hold of by a joyful sacrifice of all eartly things." Another one says: "The treasure and the pearl are pictures of the great value of the kingdom of the heavens. To possess them one has to sacrifice all his other goods" (Prof. Holtzmann). P. Lange, so well known, declares: "True Christianity is like an unexpected discovery, even in the ancient church. It is the best possession we can find, a gift of free grace. Every sinner must find and discover Christianity for himself. In order to secure possession, even of what we found with no merit of our own, we must be willing to sacrifice all; for salvation, though entirely of free grace, requires the fullest self-surrender." But enough of this. It is the general way of interpreting these two parables by making the man who sells all to obtain the treasure and the merchantman, the unsaved sinner. The Gospel, salvation, the grace of God, or as some

*Luther's Explanatory Notes on the Gospel. Page 82.

term it "religion," is, according to this, represented in the treasure and the one pearl of
great value. That such a theory is unrecon-
cilably clashing with the very heart of the
gospel is but little considered.

Gospel sermons, so-called, are preached, in
which the sinner is exhorted to give up, to sell
all, in order to become a Christian, to surrender the world and himself and *then* to find the
pearl of great value. But is this the Gospel?
We answer, No! The sinner has no sacrifice
to bring. All his trying to surrender himself
or giving up the world can never secure for
him eternal life or the grace of God. "What
must I *do* to inherit eternal life?" was spoken
by a self-righteous Pharisee, the young ruler,
and the Lord answers him, who came to Him
with the law and as under the law, accord-
ingly, and tells him to sell all he has and give
it to the poor and follow Him. But this is *not*
the gospel, but the law, which says, "Do and
live." To preach the Gospel to sinners and
tell them to *do*, to give up and to receive, is
fundamentally wrong. The Gospel of grace
does not ask of the sinner to sell all he has to
receive the grace of God and eternal life, but
the Gospel of grace offers to every sinner
eternal life as God's *gift*, a free gift, in Christ
Jesus. The Word of God, it is true, speaks of
buying; but what kind of buying is it? "Ho,
every one that thirsteth, come ye to the

waters; and he that hath *no money*, come ye, buy, and eat; yea, come, buy wine and milk *without* money and *without* price" (Is. lv:1, 2). It is buying without money and without price.

The giving up, the surrender, follows when a person is saved and has received the grace of God, but never before. We see that to teach, the man who finds the treasure is the sinner, and the sinner is to sell all to obtain the possession of Christ, or the merchantman, is the sinner who obtains a pearl, eternal life, by giving up all, is wrong teaching.* The Lord *never* meant in these parables to describe the seeking and the finding of the sinner.

The difficulty which is so apparent in the first of these two parables is but little dealt with by preachers who make the Gospel out of it. According to this wrong application the sinner would have to buy the *field* to obtain the treasure, the Gospel. What is the field? One of the above mentioned commentators makes of it "the external, worldly ecclesiasticism." This is simply a human opinion. We know what the field is. We need not to ask Dr. Luther, Lange, or any other man, what means

---

*How strange that even the simple Gospel is so little known, and there is more and more the preaching of a Gospel, which is another. A nauseating mixture of law and grace.

the field. The Lord has given us the key. "The field is the world." This is the meaning of the word field in the first two parables. Who would say that the word "field" means anything different in the fifth parable? The field is the world. If the sinner is meant by the man who buys the field, it would mean that the sinner has to buy the *world*. There is no sense whatever in giving these two parables such an application.

Again, in the two first parables a person is spoken of—the sower, the man who sowed the good seed. This Man in the first two parables is the Lord Himself. In the two parables before us the man and the merchant-man stand for the same person, and this person is identical with the man in the first and second parables; in other words, the man who bought the field and the treasure in it, and the merchantman, who sold all to obtain one pearl of great value, is the Lord Himself. It is not the unsaved seeking and finding salvation, but it is the Saviour seeking the sinner, purchasing the field, buying the treasure in it, giving up all to possess *one* pearl of great value.

As we look upon it in this light we have indeed the blessed Gospel. He, who was rich, became poor for our sakes, that by His poverty we might become rich. He, who subsisted in the form of God, emptied Himself. He came down, He gave up, He gave all and was obedi-

ent unto death, unto the death of the cross.
Both parables teach the same great truth,
Christ, the Saviour, who came to seek that
which is lost and who has purchased the field
and found in it a treasure, which is His, and
obtained one pearl of great value.

But the question arises, if this is the case,
why two parables? If the finding man and
the seeking merchantman is our Lord, why
should His work in giving up and selling all
be mentioned twice? Why is the treasure
mentioned first and then a pearl? and why is
the purchased treasure hid, while the one pearl
of great value comes evidently first into the
possession of the merchantman?

The Lord certainly speaks here of a twofold
mystery in the kingdom of the heavens and of
two different objects, which He obtained by
His work of redemption. When He mentions
the treasure hid in the field, which is His by
purchase, He means His earthly people, *Israel*.
The one pearl of great value, taken out of the
sea; the one pearl, beautiful and complete,
means the *church*, the *one* body. We have in
these two parables the mystery of Israel and the
mystery of the church; of both mysteries the
Holy Spirit witnesses in the epistles by the
Apostle of the Gentiles, to whom these mysteries were made known.

Israel is the treasure in the field. "Ye shall
be a peculiar treasure unto me above all peo-

ple; for all the earth *is* mine" (Exod. xix:5).
"For the Lord hath chosen Jacob for Himself
and Israel for His peculiar treasure" (Psa.
cxxxv:4). When He came from heaven He
found His people in the world. He bought the
whole world and with it, inclusive, the people
who are His earthly treasure. "He died for
that nation" is spoken of His blessed work
(John xi:51). However, we do not read that
He got possession of the treasure; it is rather
the thought which we get from it, that the
treasure found is hid still in the field which
He bought by so great a price, for the sake of
owning that treasure. And in this we have
the key, why this is introduced in these parables of the mysteries of the kingdom of the
heavens.

Israel is the Lord's peculiar treasure. He
has purchased His earthly people. They shall
yet be His peculiar treasure, displaying in the
earth, in the coming age, all the excellencies of
Himself. They will be a justified, a separated
and Spirit-filled people. In Balaam's prophecies the Spirit of God speaks of what Israel is
in God's eyes through the redemption work of
Jehovah. The Lord died for that nation, and
still the results of that death are not yet manifested. Israel is hid in the field, in the world.
The Lord will come again and return to the
field, the world, once more. He comes to
claim His inheritance. Then He will lift the

treasure, then He will claim His people Israel and they will rejoice in His salvation. During this age, the age of an absent Lord, Israel is kept hid in the field. This is one of the mysteries in the kingdom of the heavens. It corresponds to Rom. xi:25: "For I do not wish you to be ignorant, brethren, of this *mystery*, that ye be not wise in your own conceits, that blindness in part is happened to Israel, until the fullness of the nations be come in; and so all Israel shall be saved. According as it is written: The Deliverer shall come out of Zion; He shall turn away ungodliness from Jacob." Alas! Christendom is wise in their own conceits and has ignored, yes completely ignored this mystery. It declares that "God hath cast away His people and there is no hope for Israel." Christendom forgets that Israel is the treasure in the field, purchased by the blood, the precious blood of the Son of God, and that He, who is like a man who has gone to a far country, will come again to claim the earth and lift His peculiar treasure Israel. Much more might be said on all this, but we turn now to the meaning of the one pearl of great value.

This one pearl is the *Church*. "He loved the Church and gave Himself for it," thus it is written, and here in the parable He declares this precious truth Himself. The pearl is taken out of the sea. Way down on the dark bottom of the ocean is the shell, the house of an animal, and in this animal, by its work, the beautiful pearl is produced. A small grain of sand, we are told, imbeds itself between the animal and the shell and creates by its presence a wound in the side of the animal. Upon this miserable grain of sand the animal deposits a thin crust of a brilliant material. How often this is repeated no one can tell, one deposit after the other is made, till at last in the side of the animal there is found a most beautiful pearl, a pearl of great price, a pearl in which the colors of the rainbow of the heavens are wonderfully blended together. It is taken up and becomes the well nigh priceless jewel in the crown of some mighty monarch.

We see at once *why* our Lord used the pearl as the type of the church which He loved, and · gave Himself for it. Like Eve was taken out of the open side of Adam, so His blessed side was opened and out of that side *is* building His church. Like the pearl, the church is *one,* though composed of many countless members known to Him alone. This one pearl is *still* forming out of His side. The one pearl is still in the dark waters of the sea. How many more members will be added to this one pearl we do not know. How long it will be yet, before the Lord takes her unto Himself into the air, to adorn Himself with that precious pearl, none can tell. The church belongs to

Him, and will be with Him in the heavenlies.
Of what great value must this one pearl be to
Him, that He gave *all* for it? What glories
will He receive from the possession of that
pearl and what a beautiful object will be the
pearl in the possession of the heavenly and
eternal merchantman?

When He comes to take possession of Israel, the treasure, and of the world, His church
will be with Him. And what else might be
said of this precious parable! May we medi-
tate on it, and rejoice in that love which gave
up all to take us out of our ruin and loss un-
told, and make us the objects of His marvelous
grace.

VII.

One more parable remains, the seventh.
"Again the kingdom of the heavens is like a
dragnet cast into the sea, and which gathers
together of every kind, which when it has been
filled, having drawn up on the shore and sat
down, they gathered the good into vessels and
cast the worthless out. Thus shall it be in the
completion of the age; the angels shall go
forth and sever the wicked from among the
just, and shall cast them into the furnace of
fire; there shall be weeping and gnashing of
teeth" (verses 47-50).

This is not the Gospel net, as it is often called. After the one pearl is taken up the end of the age begins. This parable falls into the completion of the age. The dragnet is let into the sea, which, as we have seen before, represents the nations. The parable refers to the preaching of the everlasting Gospel as it will take place during the great tribulation (Rev. xiv:6, 7). The separating of the good and the bad is done by angels. All this cannot refer to the present time nor to the church, but to the time when the kingdom is about to be set up. Then angels will be used, as it is so clearly seen in the book of Revelation. The wicked will be cast into the furnace of fire and the righteous will remain in the earth for the millennial kingdom. To follow all this in detail would take us into the history of the seventieth week of Daniel. It is the same "end of the age" which is described in Matthew xxiv.

We have learned from these seven parables the mysteries of the kingdom of the heavens, beginning with the apostolic age and showing us the conditions which prevail up to its end. It is significant that the last three parables—containing, as we have seen, the mystery of Israel, the mystery of the church, and the mystery of the ending of the age—were spoken in the house to the disciples. The great multitude did not hear them, as they contain precious truths for His own, to whom alone it is given through the Spirit of God to know the mysteries of the kingdom. And so we read: "Jesus says unto them, Have ye understood all these things? They say to Him, Yea, Lord. And He said to them, For this reason every scribe discipled to the kingdom of the heavens is like a man that is a householder who brings out of his treasure things new and old" (verses 51, 52). The things old are the things revealed in the Old Testament and the new things those of the new dispensation, which are given in these parables in a nut-shell.

Upon this declaration there follows a symbolical action of our Lord. "And it came to pass when Jesus had finished these parables, He withdrew thence." The revealer of the secrets has given His revelation and now He disappears from the scene. It stands in type for His bodily absence from the earth during this age.

The end of the chapter is in full accord with the beginning and the teaching of the entire chapter. "And having come into His own country, He taught them in their synagogues, so that they were astonished, and said, Whence has this man this wisdom and these works of power? Is not this the son of a carpenter? Is not His mother called Mary, and His brethren James and Joseph, and Simeon and Juda? And His sisters, are they not all with us?

Whence then has this man all these things?
And they were offended in Him. And Jesus
said to them, A prophet is not without honor,
unless in His country and in his house. And
He did not there many works of power, because of their unbelief" (verses 54-58).

What else is all this but evidence of His full
rejection? His own knew Him not. They
speak of His earthly relations. For them He
is "this man." His Father they knew not.
They call Him "the son of the carpenter."
And thus He is rejected still by His earthly
people; and alas! many of those who call
themselves by His name during this age treat
Him no better.